To Kay
with great appreciation!

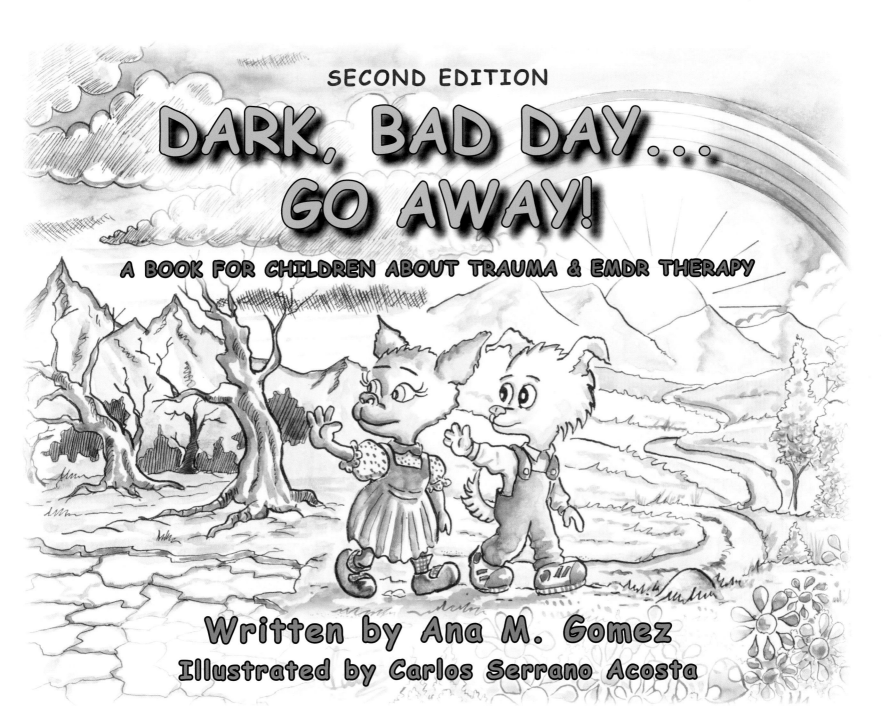

SECOND EDITION

# DARK, BAD DAY... GO AWAY!

## A BOOK FOR CHILDREN ABOUT TRAUMA & EMDR THERAPY

Written by Ana M. Gomez

Illustrated by Carlos Serrano Acosta

# INTRODUCTION

*Dark, Bad Day...Go Away* is a storybook for EMDR trained clinicians designed to explain, motivate and prepare children to use EMDR (Eye Movement Desensitization and Reprocessing) therapy.

EMDR is a psychotherapeutic approach developed by Dr. Francine Shapiro to help people heal from trauma. According to Dr. Shapiro, when a traumatic event occurs it can get locked in the brain with the original picture, sounds, thoughts, feelings and body sensations experienced during the event. Whenever a reminder of the traumatic event comes up, those pictures, thoughts, feelings, and sensations can continue to be triggered. EMDR therapy seems to stimulate the information processing system of the brain allowing traumatic memories to be unlocked, transformed and taken to an adaptive resolution. For more information on EMDR therapy go to www.emdr.com, www.emdria.org or www. emdrhap.org.

When working with traumatized children, predictability becomes essential. This book is dedicated to making EMDR trauma reprocessing more predictable and safe, and as a result, more appealing for traumatized children. *Dark, Bad Day...Go Away* can be used with children of ages 5 to 10 during the treatment planning and preparation phases of EMDR therapy.

**The *Dark, Bad Day...Go Away* storybook can help children:**

* Understand trauma, trauma symptoms and the potential outcome of not dealing with the emotions and unhealthy beliefs associated with the traumatic event.

* Understand EMDR therapy and the potential benefits of using it.

* Get acquainted with EMDR, how EMDR therapy is done and the different forms of Bilateral Stimulation (BLS).

* Be prepared for the possibility of experiencing the negative affect associated with the traumatic event so children do not stop the process when this happens. Making the process more predictable may decrease the likelihood of children stopping EMDR therapy prematurely when they experience the negative affect.

# A NOTE FOR PROFESSIONALS

**To help children understand the emotional and behavioral changes resulting from trauma as well as to identify potential targets for EMDR therapy, try the following:**

1. Ask the child what he or she thinks happened to Blaze and Nugget on the "dark, bad day."
2. Ask the child if he or she has experienced "dark, bad days."
3. Have the child draw pictures of the "dark bad days" and/or the mixed up feelings and thoughts with which he or she is currently struggling.
4. Ask the child if he or she has experienced any changes in his or her life or any feelings or thoughts similar to those of Blaze and Nugget.
5. Be aware that throughout the book the word "feelings" is referring to the emotions as well as the physical sensations. Moreover, the "mixed up stuff or bags" is referring to the dysfunctionally stored material in the brain which involves the images, thoughts, feelings, physical sensations etc.

**To help children identify more targets for EMDR trauma reprocessing try the following:**

1. When using the analogy of the "bags of mixed up feelings and thoughts" make your own bag to keep in your office. Get a pillow case, fill it with cotton and decorate it by using fabric markers. Then tie the end with a lace to make it look like a bag. This can be used to show children how difficult it could be to go through life carrying "bags of mixed up feelings and thoughts."

2. After using the analogy of the "bags of mixed up feelings and thoughts," have the child make his or her own "mixed up bag." Have the child put inside the bag "the dark, bad days" he or she has had along with the "mixed up feelings and thoughts" the child is currently experiencing. Use paper or fabric bags and cut small pieces of construction paper so that the child can draw each of the mixed up feelings and thoughts or "yucky things" that happened on the "dark, bad days". You can also use stones of different sizes as symbols for each "bad or yucky memory" or current problem. Have the child label each stone using stickers. Ask him or her to write the problem or a description of the "mixed up stuff" on the sticker. Then ask the child to put the drawings or the stones inside the "mixed up bag." After the child has finished, you will have most of the potential targets for the EMDR treatment plan.

**To help children understand the importance of doing trauma reprocessing try the following:**
1. Use specific examples from the child's life to show how different events (triggers or current stimuli) can "touch" these bags. Talk about how his or her reactions could be "too big" (exaggerated responses that are more consistent with the original trauma) or "too small" (lack of response or collapse consistent with original trauma) because the "mixed up thoughts and feelings" (dysfunctionally stored material in the brain) have been "touched" (triggered).

**When introducing and explaining EMDR therapy to children try the following:**
1. Explain how children's brains can usually chew up mixed up feelings and thoughts and make sense of yucky things when they happen by sorting them out. Sometimes though, the yucky things and the mixed up feelings and thoughts get stuck and the brain cannot do the work of sorting things out. When this happens, children can help their brains put all the pieces together, digest and chew up the "mixed up stuff" by using EMDR therapy.
2. Review some of the ways of providing bilateral stimulation (BLS) such as eye movement, tactile, and auditory stimulation. Include the butterfly hug ( Artigas ) and the EMDR puppet team. These finger puppets can make eye movement and tactile stimulation more appealing and playful for children. Explain how every night during our deepest sleep, we all move our eyes back and forth. Allow the child to explore and play with the tools and the different types of BLS. However, encourage the child to use eye movement unless he or she cannot tolerate it or strongly refuses it.
3. Prepare the child for the possibility of experiencing the "mixed up feelings and thoughts," which may happen while the child is doing eye movement or using any other type of BLS. If that happens, tell the child that it is the brain's way of letting him or her know the "mixed up stuff" is being digested and sorted out.
4. Keep the child's focus on the potential positive outcome of making more space for the positive feelings and thoughts that can begin to happen once the child gets rid of the "bags of mixed up feelings and thoughts."
5. Make sure you create realistic expectations by letting the child know the brain will digest "the mixed up stuff" one piece at a time. If children expect that all the negative affect and trauma memories are going to be reprocessed all at once, they will be disappointed if this does not happen after one session. As a result, children might not want to continue EMDR therapy, and their sense of trust and safety with the clinician might be compromised.
6. It is extremely important to assess the child's readiness to initiate trauma reprocessing. Move forward only when enough preparation has been done. The amount of preparation might vary, and it will depend on the level of environmental stability, and the child's ability to tolerate emotional disturbance.
7. When the child is ready to move forward, go through the memories identified in the "mixed up bag." Assist the child in identifying the earliest or worst memory related to the current symptoms or the one that will yield the greatest symptomatic improvement.
8. Once the target for EMDR trauma reprocessing has been identified, you can move forward with the standard procedural steps of EMDR therapy.

My name is Blaze. Nugget is my best friend. One day something really bad happened to us. It made the happy feelings in our hearts get smaller. We can't forget what happened that day. We call it the **dark, bad day**.

After the dark, bad day, we had many mixed up feelings and thoughts. We did not play or have fun together any more. We no longer felt strong, safe, or happy.

I felt angry and fought with Nugget for no reason.

Nugget was afraid and had scary dreams at night.

I got into trouble a lot and thought I was bad.

Nugget thought what happened on the dark, bad day was her fault.

Every time I remembered the
dark, bad day my heart hurt,
I had butterflies in my stomach
and I felt a lump in my throat.

One day, Maria who takes care of me, and our friend, Jimmy, asked if there was something wrong with us. They noticed that we didn't play or have fun together like we used to.

I told them about the dark, bad day and about all the sad, angry and scared feelings Nugget and I had. It was hard to talk about it, but I knew I had to tell someone I could trust.

Jimmy told us about a place called Doggie Help where something called EMDR was used to help puppies with their dark, bad days. "EMDR can help with all those mixed up feelings too," Jimmy said.

"I don't need help!" yelled Nugget angrily. "I am going to try really, really hard to forget what happened. I can do it on my own!"

Even though Nugget didn't want help, I did. I wanted to know more about EMDR and how it could help me with the sad, angry and scared feelings I had. I knew I couldn't do it by myself.

"If you keep the mixed up feelings and thoughts from the dark, bad day inside you," Jimmy said, "it is like carrying heavy bags. You are so busy carrying those mixed up feelings and thoughts that you don't have room in your heart, body and mind for good and happy feelings any more."

After thinking about what Jimmy said, Nugget and I decided to ask for help. We didn't want to carry those heavy bags from the dark, bad day any more. We made the choice to go to Doggie Help to learn about EMDR.

The next day, we went to Doggie Help. We made friends there that had dark, bad days in their lives and felt mixed up like we did.

We met Liz, the EMDR helper, who knew how to use EMDR therapy to help us.

"Nugget, have you ever eaten so much food that your stomach ached?" asked Liz.

"Yes!" Nugget said. "That happens to me a lot."

"Well....what happens in the brain when you have dark, bad days is kind of what happens in your stomach when you eat too much."

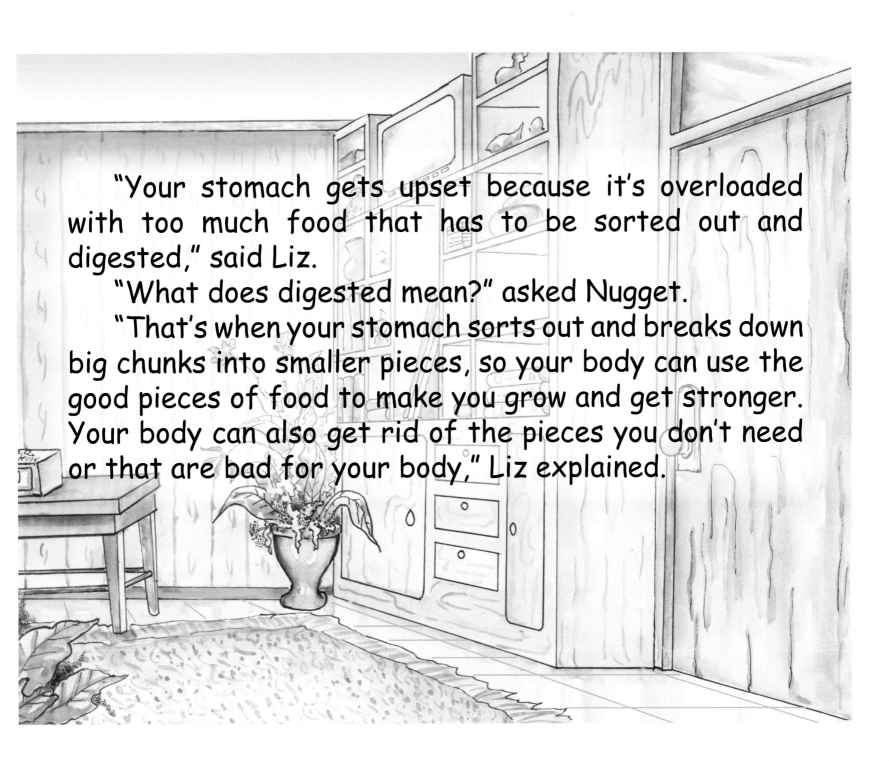

"Your stomach gets upset because it's overloaded with too much food that has to be sorted out and digested," said Liz.

"What does digested mean?" asked Nugget.

"That's when your stomach sorts out and breaks down big chunks into smaller pieces, so your body can use the good pieces of food to make you grow and get stronger. Your body can also get rid of the pieces you don't need or that are bad for your body," Liz explained.

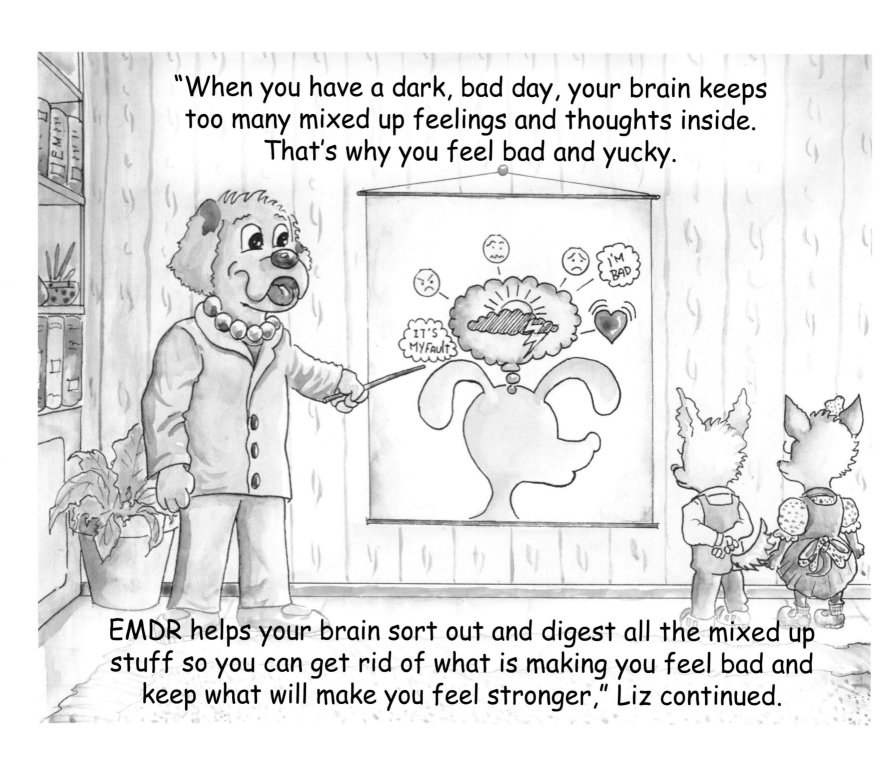

"When you have a dark, bad day, your brain keeps too many mixed up feelings and thoughts inside. That's why you feel bad and yucky.

EMDR helps your brain sort out and digest all the mixed up stuff so you can get rid of what is making you feel bad and keep what will make you feel stronger," Liz continued.

Liz showed us other ways of doing EMDR. She said she could tap our knees, shoulders, or hands back and forth.

She also taught us how to do the tapping ourselves by doing the amazing butterfly hug.

Liz had the "EMDR Puppet Team" help us move our eyes from side to side. Elizabeth the frog, Mario the moose, David the lion, and Rosie the duck were a wonderful team.

Liz told us the grown up name for EMDR but Nugget and I came up with a cool way to remember what it meant.

**E**YES

**M**OVING TO

**D**IGEST AND

**R**ECOVER!

We feel better!

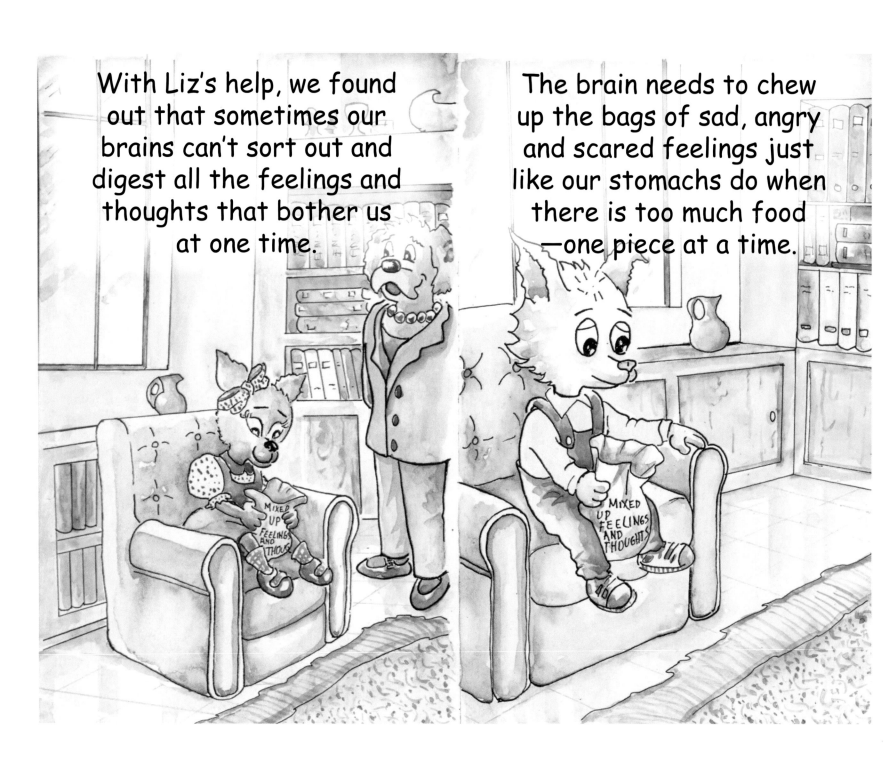

After doing EMDR for a while, I started to feel stronger and better about myself. The butterflies I felt in my stomach and the lump I felt in my throat every time I thought about the dark, bad day started to go away.

...and now Nugget has good dreams at night.

Whenever Nugget and I remember the dark, bad day, we feel brave and strong. We know we did the best we could to survive.

What happened on the dark, bad day was not our fault. We know that we are good and that we are safe now.

Nugget and I are glad we did not give up.
We are also proud that we asked for help
and most of all...that we did EMDR!

To my mother Elizabeth, the greatest gift in my life
and to my dear Blaze & Nugget

Special thanks to all the kids that allowed me
to see the world through their eyes.

Copyright © 2013 by Ana M. Gomez, M.C.
AnaGomez.org

Illustrated by Carlos Serrano Acosta
Layout by Lauren Simonetti
Edited by Kathy O'Hehir

Printed in the United States of America

ISBN 13: 978-0-9795274-0-1